SKOKIE PUBLIC LIBRARY

3 1232 00768 7850

AUG    2014

W9-DEG-313

Comparing Past and Present

# Cleaning Up

Rebecca Rissman

Heinemann
LIBRARY
Chicago, Illinois

© 2014 Heinemann Library
an imprint of Capstone Global Library, LLC
Chicago, Illinois

To contact Capstone Global Library please phone 800-747-4992, or visit our website www.capstonepub.com

All rights reserved. No part of this publication may be reproduced or transmitted in any form or by any means, electronic or mechanical, including photocopying, recording, taping, or any information storage and retrieval system, without permission in writing from the publisher.

Edited by Rebecca Rissman, Daniel Nunn, and
    Catherine Veitch
Designed by Philippa Jenkins
Picture research by Elizabeth Alexander
Production by Helen McCreath
Originated by Capstone Global Library Ltd
Printed and bound in China

17 16 15 14 13
10 9 8 7 6 5 4 3 2 1

### Library of Congress Cataloging-in-Publication Data

Rissman, Rebecca.
  Cleaning up / Rebecca Rissman.
    pages cm.—(Comparing past and present)
  Includes bibliographical references and index.
  ISBN 978-1-4329-8989-7 (hardback)—ISBN 978-1-4329-9023-7 (paperback)  1. Cleaning—Juvenile literature. 2. Cleaning—History—Juvenile literature. I. Title.
  TX324.R57 2014
  648'.5—dc23                           2013012537

## Acknowledgments

We would like to thank the following for permission to reproduce photographs: Alamy pp. 13 (© Mode Images), 15 (© Richard G. Bingham II), 23 (© Richard G. Bingham II), 23 (© Mode Images); Corbis pp. 4 (Keystone), 8 (Ted Streshinsky), 12 (Underwood & Underwood), 21 (Mike Kemp/Tetra Images); Getty Images pp. 6 (H. Armstrong Roberts), 10 (Keystone-France/Hulton Archive), 14 (Gamma-Keystone), 16 (Fox Photos/Hulton Archive), 17 (MoMo Productions/The Image Bank), 18 (Mansell/Time & Life Pictures), 20 (Gamma-Keystone), 22 (Fred Morley/Fox Photos), 23 (Mansell/Time & Life Pictures), 23 (MoMo Productions/The Image Bank); Shutterstock pp. 5 (© Yuri Arcurs), 11 (© Richard M Lee), 19 (© bikeriderlondon); Superstock pp. 7 (Cultura Limited), 9 (Glow Wellness).

Front cover photographs of two girls washing dishes in Indiana reproduced with permission of Library of Congress (Russell Lee), and a boy loading a dishwasher reproduced with permission of Shutterstock (© Monkey Business Images). Back cover photograph of children helping their mother with laundry, in 1945, reproduced with permission of Corbis (Keystone).

We would like to thank Nancy Harris and Diana Bentley for their invaluable help in the preparation of this book.

Every effort has been made to contact copyright holders of material reproduced in this book. Any omissions will be rectified in subsequent printings if notice is given to the publisher.

# Contents

Comparing the Past and Present ...... 4

Soap ................................................. 8

Washing the Dishes .......................... 10

Doing Laundry ................................. 12

Cleaning the Floors ........................... 16

Who Cleans? .................................... 18

Staying Clean ................................... 20

Then and Now .................................. 22

Picture Glossary ................................ 23

Index .............................................. 24

Note to Parents and Teachers .......... 24

# Comparing the Past and Present

Things in the past have already happened.

Things in the present are happening now.

The way people clean up
has changed over time.

The way people clean today is very different from the past.

# Soap

In the past, some people made their soap.

Today, most people buy their
soap from the store.

# Washing the Dishes

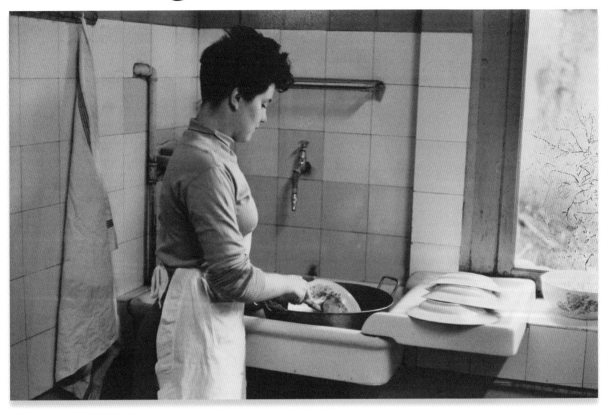

In the past, people washed
all their dishes by hand.

Today, many people wash their dishes in a dishwasher.

# Doing Laundry

In the past, people washed their clothes by hand.

Today, many people wash their clothes in a washing machine.

In the past, people hung their clothes outside to dry.

Today, many people dry
their clothes in a dryer.

# Cleaning the Floors

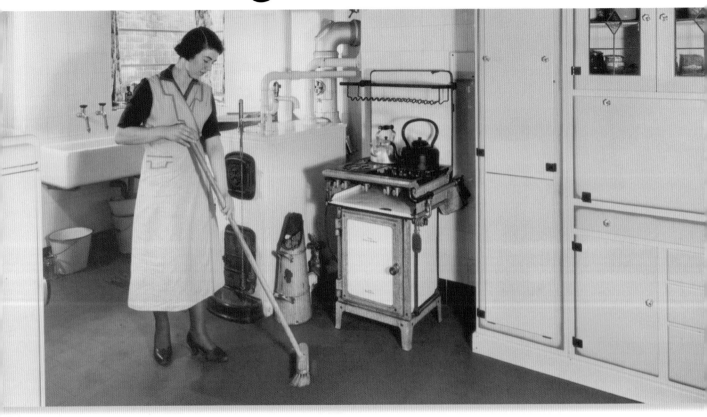

In the past, people swept or mopped their floors.

Today, many people vacuum their floors.

# Who Cleans?

servant

In the past, some families had servants to help them clean.

Today, most families clean
up after themselves.

# Staying Clean

In the past, most people did not bath much.

Today, most people have baths every day!

# Then and Now

In the past, children helped clean.
Today, children still help clean!

# Picture Glossary

 **dryer**  machine used to dry wet clothes

 **servant**  person whose job is to do things for someone else

 **vacuum cleaner**  machine used to clean floors

 **washing machine**  machine used to wash dirty clothes

# Index

bath 20, 21

dishwasher 11

dryer 13, 23

servants 18, 23

soap 8, 9

sweep 16

vacuum 17, 23

washing machine 13, 23

**Note to Parents and Teachers**

**Before reading**

Talk to children about the difference between the past and present. Explain that things from the past have already happened. Ask children to remember what they did yesterday. Then explain how that activity happened in the past. Tell children that things that are happening now are in the present.

**After reading**

- Explain to children that the way people clean has changed over time. Ask children to name three ways to clean (e.g., vacuuming, mopping, dusting, taking a bath). Then brainstorm as a group how these cleaning activities might have been different in the past.

- Ask children to turn to pages 14–15 and make a list of all the differences they see between the two photos. Keep a list of all their observations.

- Show children the photo on page 8. Explain to children that in the past, people had to make many of their own cleaning supplies. Ask children if they think life in the past might have been easier or more difficult than life today.